A Raisin in the Sun

Lorraine Hansberry

Curriculum Unit

Frances Bullock Fedor

Mary Anne Kovacs

The Center for Learning

v1.0

www.centerforlearning.org

Curriculum Unit Authors

Frances Bullock Fedor earned her M.A. from Assumption College, Worcester, Massachusetts. She also completed graduate courses at Fitchburg State College, participated in the Ecumenical Religious Studies Institute at Assumption College, and received an NDEA Grant for study of French at Goucher College. She is the coauthor of The Center for Learning novel/drama curriculum unit *The Crucible.*

Mary Anne Kovacs, who earned her M.A. at the Bread Loaf School of English at Middlebury College, Vermont, is a secondary English teacher and department head. She is also an author and coauthor of numerous curriculum units in The Center for Learning's language arts and novel/drama series, including *Nectar in a Sieve/The Woman Warrior, Anna Karenina,* and *Emma.*

Editorial Team

Mary Anne Kovacs, M.A.
Rose Schaffer, M.A.
Mary Jane Simmons, M.A.
Bernadette Vetter, M.A.

Cover Design

Susan Chowanetz Thornton, B.S.

ISBN 978-1-56077-884-4

Contents

Introduction

Lorraine Hansberry's *A Raisin in the Sun* is as popular today as it was when it first hit Broadway in 1959. Its dramatic appeal cuts across color lines in a moving portrayal of frailties, failings, and aspirations of one family. The play also faces color lines that continue to trouble us today. On Broadway in 1959, in movie form in 1961, a Broadway musical in 1973, back on Broadway in 2004, in a new movie in 2008, and with countless other productions along the way—the play clearly has staying power.

A Raisin in the Sun was born out of the author's own experience. Hansberry was born in Chicago in 1930 to a middle-class black family. When she was a child, her parents bought a home in an all-white neighborhood, so Hansberry attended predominantly white schools and encountered prejudice and bigotry from an early age. Her father fought for his civil rights in a case that went up to the Supreme Court, and he won.

In 1959 *A Raisin in the Sun* became the first Broadway play by an African-American woman. It also won the Drama Critics' Award, and thrust Hansberry into instant fame. She went on to write several other books, but became ill with cancer and met an untimely death in 1964.

The play is a real treasure for the high school teacher. The subject matter is down-to-earth, as Hansberry deftly depicts real people facing real situations. Students can easily identify with Beneatha's ambition and with her shifting enthusiasms. They can also identify with Walter, tired of his low-level job, and Ruth, caught in a relationship that seems to be failing. Everyone knows or wants to know someone like Mama—strong, rooted in traditional values, committed to her family, and determined to seek a better life.

The play is centered on a black family and has only one white character, a very disagreeable person. Depending on their own backgrounds, students may react in a variety of ways to the context. African-American students may well be able to relate their own families' experiences to those of the Younger family; many others will be equally able to identify Mama's dream with their own parents' efforts to seek a better life. Students from ethnically diverse neighborhoods will recognize that people from different backgrounds can live together in harmony. Students whose backgrounds are more limited will benefit from the opportunity to share the Younger family's pursuit of their dreams.

Teacher Notes

A Raisin in the Sun can be taught to all grades in high school, and it is useful with all levels of students, from reluctant learners to honors classes. The twelve lessons in this curriculum unit are designed to approach the play sequentially. Contents range from knowledge/comprehension activities to in-depth analysis and synthesis. Lessons include student-centered objectives, notes and background information, and step-by-step procedures, accompanied by reproducible student handouts.

The play and this unit emphasize the universal longing of people to maintain hope, even in the face of bitter opposition and disappointment, in order to fulfill dreams. Other dominant themes include the need for compassion among all members of the human family, the importance of communication in a relationship, the importance of self-esteem as a basis of maturity, and the need for tolerance, sensitivity, and acceptance toward all human beings.

The unit approaches the play as both page and stage, so students also consider theatrical elements such as set design and costuming. A film or stage version is an excellent way to end the study of the drama as a whole.

The first two lessons are introductory in nature. Lessons 3 and 4 deal with the first act; Lessons 5, 6, and 7 focus on the second act, and Lesson 8 works with the final act. If time allows, you will find it helpful to assign roles and have students read the entire play aloud together in class. To complete Lessons 9–12, students need to be familiar with the entire play. The unit also includes a test on the play.

Answers to handouts will vary unless otherwise indicated. Students may need additional paper to complete some activities.

Lesson 1
Pre-Play: "A Dream Deferred"

Objectives

- To reflect on personal dreams, aspirations, and choices

- To analyze themes, tones, and moods in poems

- To consider implications of the title of *A Raisin in the Sun*

Notes to the Teacher

Lorraine Hansberry entitled her play with an allusion to a famous poem by Langston Hughes. Most teachers are very aware of that fact; most students are not. In this lesson, students begin by looking at an assortment of poems by Langston Hughes as background for the reading of the play.

Hughes (1902–67) was born in Missouri but attended high school in Cleveland, Ohio, where he began his literary career writing for the school magazine. He spent a year at Columbia University in New York, but he finished his education at Lincoln University in Pennsylvania. There he published *The Weary Blues*, a poetry collection. Hughes went on to become a very prolific writer, producing poems, novels, short stories, plays, and nonfiction.

Hughes was a prominent writer and a leader in the Harlem Renaissance. He was one of the first black writers to demonstrate and sometimes celebrate the black experience in the United States. He was particularly concerned with other young black writers and attempted to encourage their work. His interest extended to black writers around the world, and he translated many of their poems into English.

In this lesson, students discuss dreams and aspirations. They then examine five of Langston Hughes's most popular poems: "I, Too," "Mother to Son," "Dreams," "The Negro Speaks of Rivers," and "Harlem." These and many other works by Hughes are widely available on the Internet and in books such as *The Collected Poems of Langston Hughes*, ed. Arnold Rampersad (Alfred A. Knopf, Inc., 1994).

Procedure

1. Explain to students that the next unit will involve reading and talking about a play that is concerned with people's goals and dreams. Add that considering their own goals and dreams will help them to connect with the play.

2. Distribute **Handout 1**, and direct students to complete part A. When students finish, review the handout and take a show of hands about students' responses. Allow general discussion without identifying any particular responses as good or bad.

3. Have students complete part B of the handout. Then have students share responses in large group discussion, and record dreams on the board or overhead. Note commonalities, and point out that dreams may be very specific (e.g., getting into the pre-med program at a prestigious university) or quite general (e.g., a happy family).

4. Divide students into five groups, and assign each group one of the poems by Langston Hughes. Provide hard copies or have students locate the poems on the Internet. Direct students to read the poems carefully, to provide paraphrases, to note strong images and figures of speech, to describe their own responses to the poems, and to prepare to present their findings to the class.

5. Share some of Langston Hughes's experiences with the class. (See Notes to the Teacher.) Distribute **Handout 2**, and direct students to record notes as the groups read the poems aloud and pool their insights into Hughes's style and themes.

Suggested Responses:

1. "I, Too"

> *The speaker appears to be a young boy excluded from family festivities but eager to be welcomed as both beautiful and belonging. The family symbolizes all of America, with its history of slavery and the dream of civil rights.*

2. "Mother to Son"

   Here the speaker is a mother who tells her son that life is difficult but that it is important to keep moving on, trying to reach the dream at the top of the staircase.

3. "Dreams"

   This poem asserts that we need dreams. Without them, we are broken, crippled, frozen in meaninglessness.

4. "The Negro Speaks of Rivers"

   Here the speaker is not one person, but a whole race of people, old as time and wise with experience.

5. "Harlem"

   This poem is full of figures of speech to describe possible consequences of not achieving a dream. While the other four poems seem patient and reflective, this one is edgy, with the potential of an explosion at the end.

6. Read again the first three lines of "Harlem." Then share the title of the play. Ask students to brainstorm ideas about the significance of the title.

7. If you do not plan to have the students read the play aloud in class, assign students to read the first scene in preparation for Lesson 3.

Optional Activities

1. Use the ideas developed in part B of **Handout 1** as the basis of a large scale collage or piece of art.

2. Read and report on additional poems by Langston Hughes.

Choices and Dreams

Part A.

Directions: Circle your choice to complete each statement.

1. Success means . . .	being wealthy	being happy
2. I am happiest when I think about the . . .	past	future
3. My highest priority is . . .	my social life	academic success
4. I place the highest value on . . .	personal freedom	abiding by the rules
5. In the future I hope to be . . .	wealthy	respected
6. If someone is ridiculed, I usually . . .	ignore it	defend the person
7. I get the most enjoyment out of . . .	my friends	my family
8. I see myself as a . . .	talker	listener
9. To relax, I would prefer to . . .	watch TV	go for a long walk
10. I would most hate to lose my . . .	vision	hearing
11. It is more challenging to be . . .	an engineer	a nurse
12. When I work in a group, I prefer to be . . .	the leader	quietly cooperative
13. When I have a job to do, I usually . . .	procrastinate	tackle it right away
14. Most of the time my parents and I . . .	get along well	argue with each other
15. I see myself as a . . .	giver	taker
16. To me, religion is . . .	important	unimportant
17. If I could visit another country, I would . . .	leap at the opportunity	politely decline
18. When I meet someone new, I usually . . .	introduce myself	hold back
19. I find people from other cultures . . .	frightening	interesting
20. When I experience failure, I usually . . .	give up	keep trying

Part B.

Directions: Write your name in the center circle. Then identify your dreams in the surrounding areas.

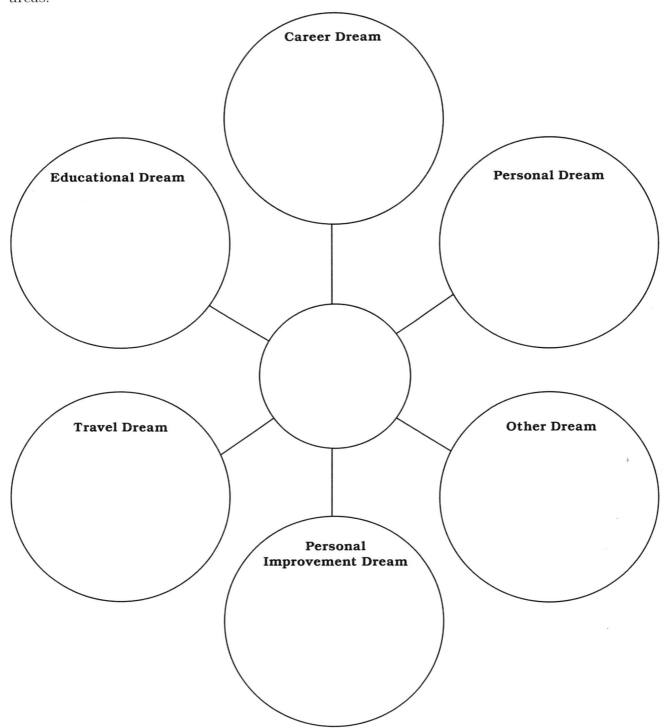

The Voice of Langston Hughes

Directions: Consider the following five poems by the famous American poet Langston Hughes. For each, record your observations about the poem and your responses to it.

Poem	Observations	Responses
1. "I, Too"		
2. "Mother to Son"		
3. "Dreams"		
4. "The Negro Speaks of Rivers"		
5. "Harlem"		

Lesson 2
Setting and Set Design

Objectives

- To visualize the stage set for *A Raisin in the Sun*

- To create a visual replication of the stage set

- To write an original description of a specific place

Notes to the Teacher

All of the play takes place in the same room, the Younger family's living room, which also serves as a bedroom for Travis. Lorraine Hansberry begins act 1 with a detailed and realistic set description. The setting is particularly important and links closely with the play's title. The environment reflects the hardship and crowded condition in which the family has lived. It also reflects the dream that Mama and her husband once shared, a dream long deferred.

Often students think of plays mainly as written literature. In fact, most plays are intended to be both "stage and page." In the theater world, set designers are extremely important people. What they do with the stage can be a critical factor in attracting audiences and holding their attention.

In this lesson, students begin with a close reading of the set description at the beginning of the play. They analyze its components. They then work in groups to create visual depictions of the set. You will want to have a variety of materials on hand: construction paper, doll house furniture (preferably worn and old), markers, computer graphics, shoe boxes, etc. Once they have worked with the set, students go on to write original descriptions, with an emphasis on use of strong images.

Procedure

1. Ask students how many have been involved in live theater. Invite open discussion of their experiences. Then ask them to brainstorm a list of people involved in producing a play. Lead them to see that many people work behind the scenes to make a play a success. One of those people is the set designer.

2. Have students read aloud the set description at the beginning of the first scene in act 1. Distribute **Handout 3,** and have students complete part A.

   Suggested Responses:

   1. *worn-out living room furniture, a threadbare carpet, a single window*
   2. *tired, worn, weariness, depressing*
   3. *The room is shabby but not messy. The doilies on the sofa show a keen desire to keep up appearances.*
   4. *In the grey of early morning, everything would look grey and somewhat dingy. All of the bright colors have long since faded out.*
   5. *Twenty years earlier the furniture would have been new and it probably would not have been necessary for someone to use the living room as a bedroom.*
   6. *The characters in the play are far from wealthy; the small apartment is crowded with five people.*

3. Read the directions for part B aloud. Point out the materials provided for students to complete the activity. Then have students divide into small groups to design stage sets. When they have finished, have groups share results with the rest of the class. Display the pieces in prominent places in the classroom.

4. Point out that Lorraine Hansberry begins her play with a description of the place setting. Distribute **Handout 4,** and have students complete part A individually. Share results as a class. Throughout the discussion, emphasize the value of very specific word and phrase choices. For example, a ceiling might be sky blue or azure; a carpet might be slime green.

5. Use part B of the handout to explain the writing assignment, and have students work with the graphic organizer to brainstorm elements of their descriptions. Set a deadline, and, if you wish, establish the criteria you will use to evaluate the writing. (You might want to limit yourself to "appeals to at least three senses," "uses vivid words and phrases," and "uses correct sentence structure.")

Name_____

Date_____

Focus on the Stage Set

Part A.

Directions: Read the description of the place setting at the beginning of the first scene in *A Raisin in the Sun*. Then answer the questions that follow.

1. What specific items are present on the stage?

2. What general terms are used to describe them?

3. Is the room we see neat and organized or sloppy and disorganized? Explain your answer.

4. What colors would dominate the stage set?

5. If the play took place twenty years earlier, how would the set be different?

6. Based on the set, what can you deduce about the characters in the play? Give specific evidence to support your answers.

Part B.

Directions: Create the set for act 1. Your work can be two-dimensional, or you may want to use a shoe box or some other tool to create a three-dimensional piece.

The Art of Description

Part A.

Directions: Read the following information. Then answer the questions that follow.

The art of description involves extensive use of imagery. Descriptions include visual images—colors and shapes, for example. Descriptions also often use sound imagery and images that appeal to the sense of touch. Some descriptions use a lot of olfactory imagery—language that appeals to the sense of smell—and some use gustatory images—appeals to the sense of taste. Descriptions of the kitchen in a bakery, for example, would appeal to all five senses.

Strong images are usually very precise and specific. A room does not simply have white walls; perhaps the walls are dingy grey, or perhaps they are gleaming white. Those are not just flowers on the table. They may be yellow rosebuds or sprigs of lilac.

Descriptions may also use figurative language. Sometimes a metaphor or a simile can convey meaning more powerfully than a simple image can. If a room smells musty, for example, you could compare it to an old tennis shoe.

1. Suppose you were describing your bedroom. What colors would you emphasize?

2. In describing an attic, what senses would you emphasize? What specific images might you include?

3. In describing a church, temple, or mosque, what smells might you emphasize? What word choices could make your readers or listeners feel as if they were actually present at the scene?

4. In describing a shopping mall, what sounds might you emphasize? Would they vary depending on the time of day?

Part B.

Directions: Select a place with which you are very familiar. Use the following graphic organizer to brainstorm images and sensations connected with that place. Then write a description in which you aim to make your readers feel as if they were right there with you.

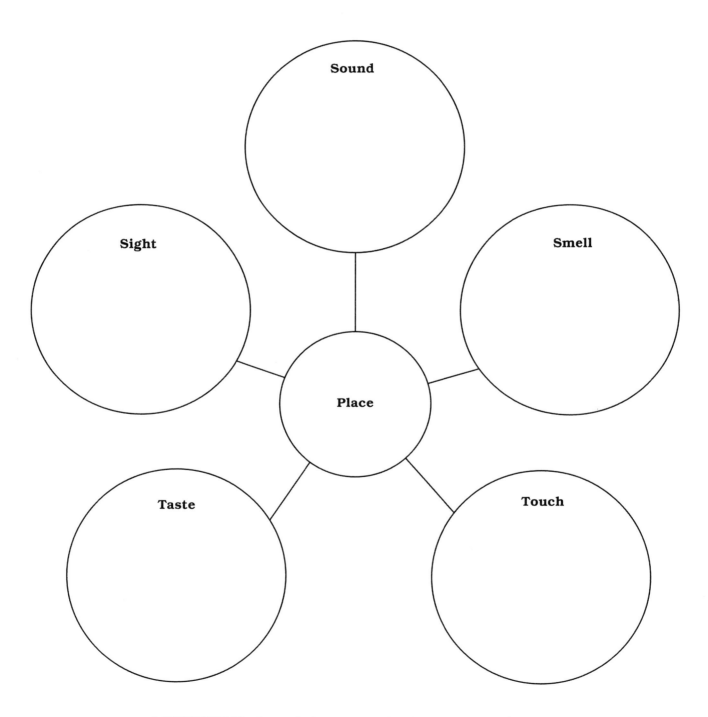

Lesson 3
Act 1, Scene 1

Objectives
- To analyze Lorraine Hansberry's initial presentation of the major characters

- To recognize causes of tension in the Younger family

- To work as a costume designer for scene 1

Notes to the Teacher
As you begin the play, you will find it useful to bring a small and somewhat bedraggled plant to the classroom and to place it in a prominent place where you can give it some attention each day prior to beginning the lesson. Allow students to gradually associate your actions to Mama's plant, a major symbol in *A Raisin in the Sun*.

The opening scene takes place on an early Friday morning in the fall and introduces the Younger family. Three generations live together in a cramped, old, and worn apartment on Chicago's south side sometime after World War II. Their environment, as well as their financial status, causes many family conflicts. Mama, the matriarch, awaits a check for $10,000 from the insurance policy of her deceased husband.

Mama Younger is a woman of strong faith rooted in traditional values. She attempts to keep harmony and unity in the family. She appreciates her late husband's hard work. Although audiences do not know it for sure until act 2, she decides to use the insurance money to buy a home for the family.

Walter Younger, Mama's son, is in his mid-thirties and weary of his job as a chauffeur. He wants to use the insurance money to go into a partnership owning a liquor store, but Mama disapproves of this. Walter's wife, Ruth, is about thirty years old and seems weighed down by disappointment. The marital relationship is teetering due to communication problems. Walter and Ruth have a son, Travis, and we later find out that Ruth is in the early stages of pregnancy.

Beneatha Younger is Walter's twenty-year-old sister. She is a college student with a burning ambition to become a doctor. She also has a history of flitting from hobby to hobby,

sometimes at considerable expense. Her brash behavior sometimes dismays her mother.

In this lesson, students read the first scene aloud. They then analyze the initial portrayals of the members of the Younger family. Finally, they design costumes appropriate for use in the scene. If you do not wish to use class time to read the scene, students will need to complete the reading prior to the lesson. For the last procedure, you may want to provide art paper and markers/colored pencils or access to computer graphics.

Procedure
1. Assign roles to class members: Ruth, Travis, Walter, Mama, and Beneatha. Have students read act 1, scene 1, aloud.

2. Ask students to surface immediate impressions of the family. Lead them to recognize tension between Walter and Ruth, between Ruth and Mama, and between Walter and Beneatha. Mama seems like a peacemaker. Travis, only about eleven years old, is beginning to develop a mind of his own.

3. Distribute **Handout 5**, and have small groups complete the exercise.

Suggested Responses:

1. *Ruth has a harried appearance. Although she is still pretty, she seems tired and worried. She is sometimes tender, sometimes abrupt with both her son and her husband. The passion between Ruth and Walter has dulled, and there is tension between them. She is proud of her contributions toward supporting the family. When Ruth faints at the end of the scene, it is evident that something is wrong.*

2. *Travis, the third generation of the Younger family, is a minor character. He seems a cooperative boy, but also is developing a kind of independence. He pushes to get the money he needs for school, and he really wants to go to work at the supermarket after school.*

3. *Walter feels that life is passing him by. His job dissatisfaction has led him to*

11

the goal of getting together with a few friends to buy a liquor store. Walter resents his mother's disapproval and his wife's apparent failure to give him moral support. He also resents Beneatha's goals and thinks she should settle for a less exalted career choice.

4. *Mama is strong, determined, caring, and protective. Although Mama is no longer young, Hansberry makes a point of emphasizing that she is still a beautiful woman. She holds fast to traditional values and religious faith, and she insists that the others in the family do the same. Mama's caring concern for the plant symbolizes her attitude toward the family. She places the needs of the family before her own.*

5. *Beneatha is energetic, quick-witted, and determined. She wants to become a doctor—a goal that involves a lot of time, effort, and money. Her independence is evident in all of her comments and actions. She can be brash, as we see in her comments about religion. She also tends to flit from hobby to hobby, perhaps looking for the interest that really suits her, but also wasting quite a bit of money.*

4. Ask students to suggest additional characteristics they see in the Younger family and to verbalize their own responses to the characters. *(Answers will vary widely, but may include that Mama tends to be a little bossy about child-rearing, Beneatha seems a very likable and perky young lady, and Walter may be too wrapped up in self-pity.)*

5. Distribute **Handout 6**, and direct students to complete the exercise.

Suggested Responses:

Ruth and Mama—*Mama's comments about Travis sometimes seem to make Ruth defensive. Mother and daughter-in-law live in very close quarters. Ruth's marriage seems on shaky ground, and her husband is Mama's son. The conflicts do not seem to endanger the relationship of the two women, at least partly because of Mama's loving nature.*

Ruth and Walter—*They seem crabby with each other, and it is evident that much of the romance has drifted out of their marriage. She is annoyed by his friends; he feels that she does not really support his ambitions. The incident involving the fifty cents Travis wants shows Walter showing off as the generous parent. Can this marriage survive? Only time will tell.*

Walter and Mama—*They may have a serious conflict over the insurance money. Ten thousand dollars comes to a poor family like this very rarely. Walter is disappointed in his own life, and he may feel that he has disappointed his mother. Mama disapproves of the liquor store idea. The ties between mother and son seem pretty strong, however.*

Walter and Beneatha—*They have conflict in a nonthreatening way as brothers and sisters often do. They quarrel about the money and about their goals, but no danger seems incipient in their disagreements.*

6. Remind students that the play is a "page" experience, but it is also a "stage" experience. Divide the class into small groups, and assign each group one member of the Younger family. Ask students to serve as costume designers for the scene and to determine all aspects of the characters' physical appearances. If necessary, prompt the class with questions such as the following:

- Travis crawls out of his bed on the sofa. Would he be wearing sweats? a worn-out pair of Mickey Mouse pajamas?

- Would Ruth's hair be neatly combed, or would it be wrapped in a towel?

- Ruth might be wearing a worn-out robe and slippers, but how do you see Beneatha?

- Does Mama come into the room in a bathrobe, or would she get dressed for the day before entering?

7. When groups have finished, have them share decisions with the rest of the class, and conduct a discussion based on their ideas. Emphasize that there is no one right way to present each character, but specific decisions about costumes and hairstyles can have a big impact on the production as a whole.

Name_____

Date_____

Meet the Main Characters

Directions: The first scene of *A Raisin in the Sun* introduces the Younger family. Find actions and dialogue that show the following characteristics.

Character/ Characteristics	Evidence from the Play
1. Ruth	
a. Disappointed	
b. Loving	
c. Nagging	
d. Proud	
2. Travis	
a. Obedient	
b. Intelligent	
c. Motivated	
3. Walter	
a. Frustrated	
b. Ambitious	
c. Self-centered	
d. Proud	

Name_____

Date_____

Character/ Characteristics	Evidence from the Play
4. Mama	
a. Domineering	
b. Optimistic	
c. Caring	
d. Protective	
e. Proud	
5. Beneatha	
a. Independent	
b. Searching	
c. Ambitious	
d. Brash	

Name_____

Date_____

Causes of Conflict

Directions: In the first scene of *A Raisin in the Sun*, we sense several significant conflicts among the members of the Younger family. Identify the issues and concerns at the root of the following areas of tension. Then indicate how serious you think the conflicts are.

Ruth and Mama

Ruth and Walter

Walter and Mama

Walter and Beneatha

Lesson 4
Act 1, Scene 2

Objectives
- To analyze the characters' interactions and motivations
- To research Joseph Asagai's native country, Nigeria

Notes to the Teacher
The second scene takes place the next morning, a Saturday, and complicates the basic relationships introduced at the beginning of the play. One of the reasons for Ruth's frustration becomes clear: she is pregnant, and it is evident that she is considering an abortion.

The entire family is anxiously aware of the imminent arrival of the check. Walter is obviously determined to use it to pay for his share of the liquor store. Mama does not reveal her exact intentions for the money, although she does mention the dream of getting out of the apartment into a house, but she rejects the proposal about the liquor store. Meanwhile, the women are engaged in heavy-duty Saturday morning cleaning and a determined effort to keep the cockroaches out. The arrival of Joseph Asagai introduces an entirely new dimension into the play. A college student from Nigeria, he is clearly attracted to Beneatha and proud of his African heritage.

The scene ends on a dark note. Walter wants to talk about nothing except his liquor store aspirations. Ruth needs to talk with him about her pregnancy. Mama wants Walter to listen to Ruth and to know that Ruth is considering aborting the baby. When Walter walks out at the end of the scene, we experience a kind of cliffhanger. What will happen next?

In this lesson, students read the scene aloud. (If you do not have time for this, students will need to have completed the reading as homework.) They then use a study guide to review their understanding of the first act as a whole and consider the mounting frustrations among the characters. They go on to an exercise involving vocabulary in the first two scenes. Finally, they focus on Asagai and the influence he brings to the play. For the final procedures, students will need access to print resources and the Internet in order to research information about Nigeria.

Procedure
1. Assign roles (Travis, Mama, Beneatha, Walter, Ruth, Asagai), and have students read the second scene aloud.
2. Distribute **Handout 7**, and have small groups complete the exercise.

Suggested Responses:

1. *Walter is very frustrated with his menial position as a chauffeur and with his home life. He feels that no one in the family really understands or supports him.*

2. *Walter hopes that Ruth can talk Mama into allowing Walter to use the insurance money to buy into the ownership of a liquor store.*

3. *Walter feels that Ruth should give him more support and affirmation.*

4. *Walter dreams of quitting his job and becoming a business success. Perhaps he is overly optimistic in seeing co-ownership of the store as a way to success.*

5. *Beneatha dreams of becoming a doctor—a dream that requires a lot of time, hard work, and money.*

6. *The two have normal sibling rivalry. Walter also resents Beneatha's dream and wishes she would settle for a less exalted career, one that he would see as more suitable for a woman.*

7. *Ruth is easily irritated when Mama tries to take over motherly roles with Travis.*

8. *Mama is a religious woman who does not see running a liquor store as a good goal. She probably also realizes that Walter does not have much business experience.*

9. *Ruth suggests that Mama use the money to take a vacation; Mama rejects the idea. She is more interested in the family and thinks it would be nice to buy a house.*

10. *Big Walter was Mama's husband. Years ago, when they acquired the apartment, they had big dreams. He seems to have been a hard-working man who was very dedicated to his family.*

11. *Beneatha says that she is tired of hearing about God. This upsets Mama, who will not have that kind of talk in her home.*

12. *Ruth seems depressed. She is well aware of the cramped apartment, the limited financial resources, and the shaky state of her relationship with her husband.*

13. *Asagai is a college student from Nigeria. He is romantically attracted to Beneatha. He also seems amused by her, perhaps a little condescending. Beneatha likes him, but she also wishes to be independent. Beneatha has been dating George Murchison, but she does not seem to be very serious about him.*

14. *Walter is so frustrated at feeling stuck and powerless in his life. He feels doomed.*

15. *Mama seems to expect Walter to provide support and encouragement to his wife. Instead, he walks out the door, probably to go get drunk. The plot could go many directions from this point. Will Walter get killed in a bar fight? Will he pick up with another woman? Will Ruth pack up and move out with Travis? Will Mama give in and allow Walter to use the insurance money?*

3. Point out that Joseph Asagai adds something new to the play. He comes from a faraway country in Africa and provides a kind of exotic, cosmopolitan influence. Ask students the following questions:

   a. What gift does Asagai give to Beneatha?
   (*a traditional Nigerian costume, including dress and head piece*)

   b. What does he say about her hair?
   (*He sees straightening it as a kind of mutilation of her natural beauty.*)

   c. What is assimilationism?
   (*the idea that minority cultures should abandon their own ethnic traditions and try in every way to fit in with the majority*)

4. Distribute **Handout 8**, and review the directions for part A. If necessary, point out root words, and explain that students may not find the adverb *forlornly* in the dictionary, but they will find the adjective *forlorn*. Ask small groups to collaborate to find definitions and to complete part B of the exercise. Point out that some of the words are closely related. For example, *vain* and *futile* could be viewed as synonyms. A person in a state of depression might speak forlornly.

Suggested Responses:

Part A.

1. useless
2. accusation
3. frustrated
4. cleared of blame
5. energetically
6. great pain
7. not obviously
8. weak
9. in a sneaky way
10. useless
11. noisy
12. sadly
13. depression
14. questioning
15. disbelief

Part B.

1. indictment
2. anguish
3. unobtrusively
4. quizzical
5. raucous
6. exasperated
7. futile
8. feeble
9. furtively
10. incredulity

18

11. *dejection*

12. *vindicated*

13. *vigorously*

14. *forlornly*

15. *vain*

5. Distribute **Handout 9**, and have students use the Internet and print resources to research Nigeria.

Suggested Responses:

1. *Nigeria is on Africa's west coast and is bordered by Chad, Benin, Niger, and Cameroon. The Atlantic Ocean is to the west, the Niger River runs through it, and it has rain forests.*

2. *Like much of Africa, Nigeria was an object of European imperialism. The first European explorers arrived at the end of the fifteenth century. During the second half of the nineteenth century, it was claimed by England. It finally won independence in 1960, but the country has been far from peaceful.*

3. *English is the official language, but there are also indigenous languages, dialects such as Yoruba and Ibo.*

4. *1959 was the eve of Nigerian independence. Asagai represents a country optimistic in expectation of great new things.*

5. *Elections in 2007 sought to build a base for stability, but conflicting forces within the country make that goal difficult.*

6. *Nigeria is a big force in the world music industry; the sounds of Nigerian rock music will be very familiar to many students.*

7. *A glance at Nigerian recipes on the Internet will reveal entrées similar to many of our own.*

8. *The main religions are Islam and Christianity; the conflict between the two is a source of some of the national unrest. There are also traditional African religions.*

9. *Gender roles are rather strictly limited to traditional ways.*

10. *Students will find many elaborate costumes made of rich and colorful materials. The Yoruban gown and headdress would give Beneatha an exotic and strangely glamorous look.*

Name_____

Date_____

Act 1: Questions for Discussion

Directions: Use the following questions to review and analyze the first act of *A Raisin in the Sun*.

1. Why is Walter such an angry person?

2. At the beginning of the play, why does Walter want Ruth to talk to Mama?

3. Why is Walter resentful toward Ruth?

4. What is Walter's dream? Do you think it can come true?

5. What is Beneatha's dream? Do you think it can come true?

6. Why does Walter pick on his sister?

7. What causes friction between Mama and Ruth?

8. Why is Mama opposed to the liquor store?

9. What suggestion does Ruth make to Mama about the use of the money? How does Mama respond?

10. Who was Big Walter? What do we learn about him?

11. What causes the argument between Mama and Beneatha at the end of the first scene?

12. Why does Ruth consider having an abortion?

13. Who is Joseph Asagai? What seem to be his attitudes toward Beneatha? What are her attitudes toward him? Who is George Murchison?

14. How does Walter describe his frustration to Mama?

15. How does Walter disappoint Mama at the end of the first act? What do you think will happen next?

Name_____

Date_____

Act 1: Vocabulary Development

Part A.

Directions: *A Raisin in the Sun* is not filled with difficult words, but Lorraine Hansberry does use some vocabulary that may be unfamiliar to you. The following words are listed in the order in which they appear in the first act. Define them based on both context and a dictionary.

1. vain

2. indictment

3. exasperated

4. vindicated

5. vigorously

6. anguish

7. unobtrusively

8. feeble

9. furtively

10. futile

11. raucous

12. forlornly

13. dejection

14. quizzical

15. incredulity

Part B.

Directions: Fill in the blanks in the following sentences with the best choices from part A.

1. The Grand Jury issued an _____ against the defendant.

2. The death of a loved one causes great _____.

3. I was late, so I tried to enter the classroom _____.

4. Tim's _____ expression indicated that he was confused.

5. The _____ cries of crows emanated from the woods.

6. We were _____ by the long wait at the airport.

7. Our efforts to get the car out of the snowdrift were _____, so we had to call a tow truck.

8. The newborn kitten was too _____ to walk to its mother.

9. The thief glanced _____ around before he crept in the window.

10. When I heard that we won the lottery, my first reaction was complete _____.

11. The look of _____ on my dog's face convinced me that he needed a treat.

12. The attorney proved that all of the evidence _____ his client.

13. To clean the basement floor, you need to scrub much more _____.

14. The mourners at the funeral gazed _____ at the coffin.

15. After a three-hour wait for the bus, I knew that all of my efforts to arrive on time for the performance were in _____.

Asagai's Country: Nigeria

Directions: Use the Internet and print materials to discover information about Joseph Asagai's native country.

1. Where is Nigeria? What are its neighbors? What are its main geographical features?

2. What are some major events in the history of Nigeria?

3. What languages are spoken in Nigeria?

4. *A Raisin in the Sun* was first staged in 1959. What was the situation in Nigeria then?

5. What is the situation in Nigeria now?

6. What does Nigerian music sound like?

7. What kinds of foods are popular in Nigeria?

8. What are the main religions?

9. What roles are usually assigned to men and women in Nigeria?

10. Find examples of traditional Yoruba women's dresses and head pieces. Select one that you would choose for Beneatha to wear if you were staging the play. Place a visual reproduction of it on the back of this paper.

Lesson 5
Act 2, Scene 1

Objectives
- To identify characters and events in the scene
- To analyze the interaction between Beneatha and George Murchison
- To note the deteriorating relationship between Ruth and Walter and the cataclysmic effect of Mama's announcement

Notes to the Teacher
This scene takes place later the same day and begins with a colorful performance by Beneatha and a rather drunk Walter. George Murchison's arrival to pick up Beneatha for a theater date interrupts them. The audience immediately sees that Murchison, a true assimilationist, is the antithesis of Asagai. Walter's resentment and frustration are evident in every word he says, and they reach a new high when Mama returns home and announces that she has purchased a house—in a white neighborhood. Walter's parting words, "So you butchered up a dream of mine," leave both Mama and the audience deep in thought.

In this lesson, students begin with an oral reading of the scene, and they attempt to dramatize Beneatha's and Walter's performance at the beginning of the scene. They then examine the interchange between Beneatha and George, with a focus on their differing views of heritage and assimilationism. They go on to examine the conversation between Ruth and Walter and the effect of Mama's announcement.

Procedure
1. Have students complete an oral reading of the scene, which includes Beneatha, Ruth, Walter, George, Mama, and Travis. (Consider asking students with skills in dramatics and music to perform the roles of Beneatha and Walter at the beginning of the scene. Beneatha needs to dance and sing, and Walter needs to be prepared for some flamboyant acting.) Point out Ruth's wry comments.

2. Distribute **Handout 10**, and have small groups complete the exercise.

   Suggested Responses:

   Beneatha and George are prickly around one another throughout their interaction. George mocks her Nigerian dress and is critical of her new natural haircut. Beneatha accuses him of being an assimilationist, leading to an argument about African culture. George seems to be a very smug young man, and Beneatha, despite her outspoken responses, seems to be somewhat vulnerable.

3. Point out that the conversation between Beneatha and George is followed by one between Ruth and Walter. Ask students to review the dialogue and to state the dominant theme of their interaction. (*A gap has opened between them, and neither knows what to do about it. The romance is gone.*)

4. Point out that Mama's entrance interrupts their conversation, and she makes an astounding announcement. What is it? (*She has purchased a modest house—one in an all-white neighborhood.*) Ask students to describe the other characters' reactions. (*Ruth seems delighted, Travis accepting, and Walter outraged.*)

5. Distribute **Handout 11**, and have students complete the exercise individually. Then conduct a discussion based on responses.

   Suggested Responses:

   1. *Walter feels totally unsupported and misunderstood. He really wants money to invest in a liquor store—and Mama does not approve of that idea.*

   2. *He seems to want to express his rage and frustration, but his word choices are also intended to hurt Mama.*

   3. Butchered *implies savagery and ferocity, even criminal intent.*

   4. *We know that Mama cares deeply about her family, and Walter's words are sure to have hurt her. Will she give up on the*

house and let Walter have the money after all? Will she insist on an apology? Will she try to reason with him?

5. *Encourage students to share only butchered dreams that are now safe areas of conversation for them. Examples may include divorce in the family, not making a team, the breakup of a romance, not being accepted by a school or an employer, etc. Students may note that sometimes an explosion is therapeutic; sometimes it may cause disaster.*

6. *Only time can tell if the loss of a dream is, in the end, harmful or helpful. Maybe it was simply the wrong dream, or an unattainable one.*

Beneatha and George Murchison

Directions: In act 1, we observed Beneatha's interaction with one young man, Joseph Asagai. In the first scene of act 2, we see her with another friend, George Murchison. Review their conversation, and complete the following exercise. Record dialogue that reflects the following responses, and indicate the causes that precipitate the responses.

Response	Dialogue	Cause
1. Irritation		
2. Confrontation		
3. Resentment		
4. Sarcasm		
5. Anger		

Name_____

Date_____

"So You Butchered Up a Dream of Mine . . ."

Directions: Review the closing lines in the first scene of act 2. Use the following questions to process Walter's response to Mama's purchase of the house.

1. Why is Walter so upset? What does he want?

2. What do you see as his purpose in his last comments to Mama?

3. *Butchered* is a strong word. How does it impact both Mama and the audience?

4. The scene ends with Mama deep in thought. What do you think she will do next? Why?

5. Have you ever had a dream that you felt was butchered? Describe your experience. (If this has never happened to you, describe the experience of someone you know who has been badly disappointed.) Did you (or the other person) explode, as Walter does?

6. Was the experience, in the long run, a good one or a bad one? Explain.

Lesson 6
Act 2, Scene 2 ¹⁴

Objectives
- To recognize the deteriorating relationships evident in the play
- To review and practice the conventions of the personal letter
- To recognize the impact of money on people's dreams

Notes to the Teacher
This scene takes place a few weeks later, with the family deeply involved in packing for the big move. Beneatha returns from a date with George and decides she is through with him, a decision that usually does not surprise students after the analysis completed during the study of the first scene in act 2. Mrs. Johnson (a neighbor and a character not included in the first version of the play) comes in full of dire comments about the coming move.

A phone call from Walter's employer reveals that he has not been going to work. Students see the answer to one of the last questions they considered in the previous lesson. Mama relents and gives Walter the $6,500 she has left, asking him to bank $3,000 for Beneatha, but allowing him to do what he wants with the rest. The scene ends with a blissfully happy Walter describing his vision of a happy future to Travis.

In this lesson, students begin with an oral reading of the scene. They then focus on the demise of the relationship between Beneatha and George. Next they consider what Walter has been doing with his days, and they examine his response to Mama's gift.

Procedure
1. Have students complete an oral reading of the scene. Voices include George, Beneatha, Mama, Ruth, Mrs. Johnson, Walter, and Travis.

2. Ask students why Beneatha decides to break up with George. (*She spurns his attempts at kisses, and he reacts by criticizing her moodiness. Then he makes comments that indicate his totally pragmatic attitude toward education—a far cry from Beneatha's idealism. Beneatha concludes that he is simply a fool.*)

3. Review the conventions used in a personal letter.
   - At the top right of the page the letter-writer should put his or her address and the date.
   - The letter should have an appropriate salutation, e.g., "Dear Fred."
   - Paragraphs should be indented, and the whole letter should look neat and readable.
   - After the body of the letter, to the right, should go an appropriate closing, e.g., "With love," followed by the writer's signature.

4. Distribute **Handout 12**, and have students complete the exercise individually. (Note: You may want to assign roles so that all four types of letters are used.) When students have finished writing, have them share letters in small groups. Then invite some to read the work aloud to the entire class.

5. Point out that Mrs. Johnson plays a very minor role, and some people argue that she can be left entirely out of the play with no loss to the dramatic action. Ask volunteers to describe her. (*She is a nosy, gossipy neighbor. Beneatha obviously has no use for her.*)

6. Conduct a discussion based on the following topics.
   a. Mama surprises Walter—and many audience members, as well—when she gives him the money after all. What reasons do you think she has for this decision?
   (*His comment about butchered dreams and her desire for his well-being play a role.*)

   b. What are Mama's specific directions for the use of the money?
   (*$3,000 is to be banked for Beneatha's education; the rest is available to Walter.*)

   c. Do you think Mama's decision will restore peace to the Younger family?
   (*Some students may sense that Walter will not do well with the money.*)

29

7. Ask students to reread the scene's closing monologue. Point out that Walter here reveals his pipe dream of the life he would like to have. Ask students to brainstorm a list of words that represent elements of his dream (*respect, authority, a classy car for himself and one for Ruth, servants, an affectionate wife, and a son of whom he can be proud*).

8. Distribute **Handout 13**, and have students complete the exercise. Keep an informal atmosphere so that students can share ideas. Then conduct a discussion based on students' responses, and note ways in which their dreams are like and unlike Walter's. You may want to extend this activity into an essay assignment.

Name_____

Date_____

A Personal Letter

Directions: Imagine yourself in one of the following situations. Try to totally identify with the character in the play. Then write the designated letter, using all of the conventions of a correct personal or "friendly" letter.

Option 1

You are Beneatha Younger, and you have decided that George Murchison is a fool. You do not intend to continue dating him. You have known him for a long time, and, besides a few sarcastic comments, he has always treated you well. You decide it is only fair to explain your decision, and you decide to do so in a letter.

Option 2

You are George Murchison, and Beneatha has you really confused. At the end of your last date, the two of you had an argument about education, and not long ago you quarreled about Africa. Recently you found her wearing African attire, and she cut her beautiful hair and is now wearing it in a short, kinky style. You decide to write her a letter in an attempt to mend your relationship.

Option 3

You are Joseph Asagai. You are strongly attracted to Beneatha, but you know she is also dating another man. She is very independent, unlike the subservient women back home in Nigeria. Sometimes you think she is a little immature, but still delightful. You would like a serious relationship with her, but you know you intend to return to your native country. You decide to write Beneatha a letter explaining your thoughts.

Option 4

You are Beneatha Younger, and you have just broken up with George Murchison. You would like to pursue a closer relationship with Joseph Asagai, but you also are determined to complete your education and become a doctor. Your African ancestry is a source of fascination and pride to you, and you know Asagai intends to return to Nigeria after he completes his education. You decide to write him a letter to share your thoughts.

A Raisin in the Sun
Lesson 6
Handout 13

Name_____

Date_____

My Dream for the Future

Directions: Walter Younger's dream for the future includes his career, his possessions, and his family. What if you came into enough money to make all or most of your dreams come true? What would you aim for?

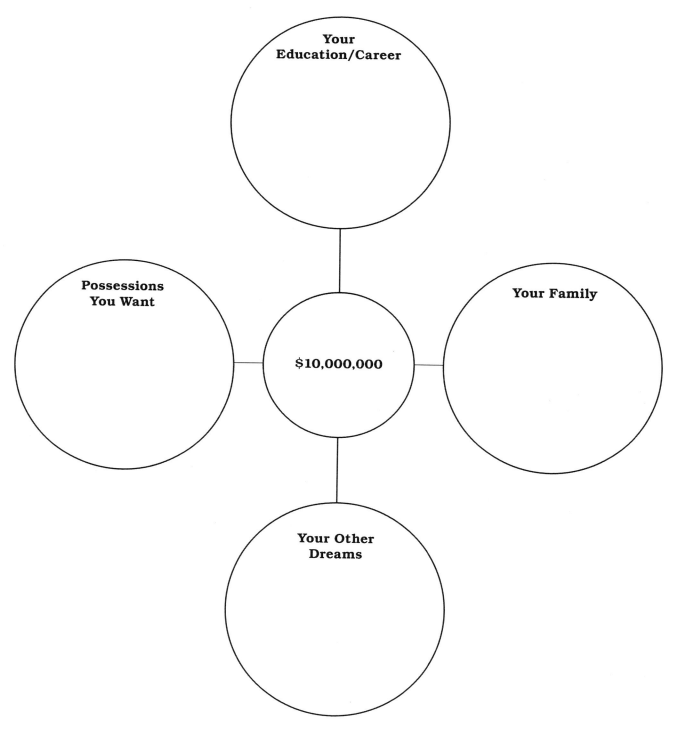

Lesson 7
Act 2, Scene 3

Objectives
- To recognize the major problems that arise during the scene
- To see how act 2 moves the play's action forward
- To predict the final outcome for the Younger family

Notes to the Teacher

This scene occurs a week later, on moving day, and begins happily. The visit of Karl Lindner, the only white character in the play, interrupts. His purpose is clear: to deter the Younger family from moving to Clybourne Park, where they are not wanted. Mama prepares her plant for the move, and the family presents her with a gift of gardening tools. Then the really bad news comes: Walter's would-be business partner, Willy, has run off with all of the investment money. The scene ends with Mama's prayer for strength.

This lesson begins with an oral reading of the scene. Students then reflect on the bad news in the scene. The white people at Clybourne Park do not want the Youngers to move in; Walter has lost $6,500. Students then complete a study guide to review act 2 as a whole, and they go on to study vocabulary based on the act. They conclude by researching the play's historical background. To complete the final procedure in the classroom, students will need access to the Internet.

Procedure

1. Have students complete an oral reading of the scene. Roles include Ruth, Beneatha, Mr. Lindner, Walter, Mama, Travis, and Bobo.

2. Point out that the scene presents two impediments to the family's move. Ask students to identify them.

   Suggested Responses:

   1. *Mr. Lindner makes it clear that the people who already live in Clybourne Park do not see racial integration as a goal. The Youngers simply are not wanted there. Earlier the play mentioned violence*

against African Americans who moved into white neighborhoods, so there is always the possibility that awful things could happen to the Younger family. At the very least, it is not comfortable to move into a hostile environment.

2. *Bobo brings the terrible news that Willy has absconded with the money intended to buy the liquor store. Now Walter's dream has surely been butchered. Walter must admit that he did not put Beneatha's share of the money in the bank; he lost all of it. Perhaps Beneatha's dream, too, will die.*

3. Distribute **Handout 14**, and direct small groups to use it to review act 2.

   Suggested Responses:

   1. *Throughout the play so far, Walter is moody and frustrated when things do not go his way. Once Mama gives him the money, he becomes almost euphoric. When Willy absconds with the money, Walter is devastated. Ruth is despondent over the failing marriage relationship; when Walter warms toward her, she becomes happy.*

   2. *Asagai despises assimilationism, and George is a total assimilationist. George is upset with Beneatha when he finds her in African dress; Asagai has a high regard for that same dress. Asagai is an intellectual and an idealist, while George has no interest in intellectual pursuits He is, as Beneatha says, a shallow character, primarily interested in material success. Asagai's cultural pride and desire to help his country make him an admirable character.*

   3. *Mrs. Johnson was not in the first productions of the play, and one could argue that she can be omitted easily. She does, however, add the insight that the Younger family's black neighbors may be no more in favor of the move than Mr. Lindner is. Her motives are ambiguous—perhaps a combination of greed, selfishness, envy, empathy, and fear.*

4. *Mr. Lindner appears to be a polite, proper, fearful little representative of the white society at Clybourne Park. He does not appear to be a mean or vindictive man—just blind, determined, and completely without insight. He represents a culture that is bigoted, prejudiced, and blindly self-protective.*

5. *Prometheus is a god in Greek mythology. He stole fire and gave it to humans, thus empowering them, and earned retribution by Zeus. Prometheus was chained to a mountaintop where an eagle came daily to eat at his liver. George is mocking Walter's frustrated aspirations.*

6. *The gifts of the gardening tools and hat indicate the family's respect and affirmation of Mama's dreams. Despite all of the bickering, they love and admire her.*

7. *Walter is devastated. He has not only lost his own dream, but he has also destroyed the dreams of the rest of the family. Mama is at first shocked and disillusioned, but she remains a solid foundation for the family. She is disturbed that both of her children seem to be losing their dreams. Beneatha seems to be left speechless. Later we will see that she totally blames Walter and feels that she no longer has any use for him.*

8. *Will the family give up on the house? Will Walter leave the family for good? Will Beneatha use Asagai as a way to flee the whole situation, or will she turn to George as a possible source of income to finish her education?*

4. Distribute **Handout 15**, and have small groups complete the vocabulary exercise.

Suggested Responses:

Part A.

1. *like a flirt*
2. *overly proud*
3. *an overused phrase*
4. *watches carefully*
5. *sadly*

6. *in a threatening way*
7. *uncertainly*
8. *enmity*
9. *motion*
10. *spirited*
11. *refuse curtly*
12. *disaster*
13. *shrill*
14. *in a friendly way*
15. *ridiculous*

Part B.

1. *arrogant*
2. *catastrophe*
3. *menacingly*
4. *ludicrous*
5. *scrutinizes*
6. *coquettishly*
7. *strident*
8. *cliché*
9. *hostility*
10. *rebuff*
11. *tentatively*
12. *exuberant*
13. *momentum*
14. *amiably*
15. *plaintively*

5. Point out that the play is set in a definite historical context. Distribute **Handout 16**, and direct students to complete the research. Then ask students to pool results in a class discussion.

Suggested Responses:

1. *Hansberry wrote about a situation she knew well. She grew up in Chicago in a middle-class African-American family. In 1938 her father purchased a home in an all-white neighborhood and moved the family from the south side to that location.*

2. *Hansberry's parents were, in a way, ahead of their time. The civil rights movement is usually associated mostly with the 1950s and 1960s, as black*

Americans fought for equality. Remarkable leaders emerged during this time. Some, like Dr. Martin Luther King Jr., espoused nonviolent protest. Others saw violence as a necessary option.

3. *Most of the demonstrations in Chicago during the 1950s involved whites protesting against black people striving for upward mobility.*

4. *Many cities in the South will come to mind, but there were also public uprisings in northern cities, including Detroit and New York City. Although there was also civil unrest in Chicago, some commentators state that, considering the size of the city and its demographics, there were surprisingly few serious incidents.*

5. *In Chicago, as in many cities, the neighborhood originated with white settlers. As they became increasingly prosperous, they moved away from the city. By the time of the play, the south side was considered an urban African-American area. In Chicago, the races were separated not by law, but by practice.*

6. *The play elicits empathy for the Younger family. It could help white audiences to a whole new perspective on the racial situation.*

7. *Depending on the area in which you teach, students may have very different views on this subject. You may want to widen the discussion beyond African Americans to include other groups. Emphasize that people often fear change and find it difficult to accept those with different cultural and religious backgrounds than their own.*

Name_____

Date_____

Act 2: Discussion Questions

Directions: Use the following questions to discuss the events in the second act.

1. How would you explain the ups and downs in Walter's moods? Ruth's?

2. Compare and contrast Joseph Asagai and George Murchison.

3. What does Mrs. Johnson add to the play?

4. Describe Mr. Lindner. What does he represent?

5. In act 2, scene 1, George says to Walter, "Good night, Prometheus!" Who is Prometheus? What does George mean?

6. What do the family's gifts to Mama reveal about their attitudes toward her?

7. Does the loss of the money surprise you? Describe the reactions of the characters.

8. Only one short act is left in *A Raisin in the Sun*. What do you expect to happen?

Name_____

Date_____

Act 2: Vocabulary Development

Part A.

Directions: The following words are presented in the order in which they appear in the second act. Use both context and a dictionary to define them.

1. coquettishly

2. arrogant

3. cliché

4. scrutinizes

5. plaintively

6. menacingly

7. tentatively

8. hostility

9. momentum

10. exuberant

11. rebuff

12. catastrophe

13. strident

14. amiably

15. ludicrous

Part B.

Directions: Complete each of the following sentences with an appropriate word from part A.

1. _____ people have no humility.

2. The stock market collapse was a financial _____ for many families.

3. The dog snarled _____ at the pedestrian.

4. We laughed at the _____ antics of the slapstick comedian.

5. The accountant _____ each tax form with a careful eye.

6. The girl peeked _____ from behind her fan.

7. The _____ sound of the fire engine warned drivers to pull to the side of the road.

8. "Cool as a cucumber" is an example of a _____.

9. The ambassadors will meet to try to minimize the _____ between the two countries.

10. I don't mean to _____ your kind offer, but I really do not want to see that movie.

11. Schedule my appointment _____ for noon, and I will call to confirm it later.

12. The cheerleaders' _____ performance got all of the fans excited.

13. Now that the business has some forward _____, I think we are headed for a lot of success.

14. Bill strolled _____ among all of his friends at the party.

15. The performer sang _____ about star-crossed lovers.

Name_____

Date_____

Historical Background

Directions: A *Raisin in the Sun* takes place during the middle of the twentieth century. This was the very beginning of a major move for equality in America. Use the Internet to find information about the historical accuracy of the play.

1. Where did Lorraine Hansberry grow up? Who were her parents? What parts of her own life did she put into the play?

2. What was the civil rights movement?

3. During the 1950s in Chicago, there were racial demonstrations. What was typical about them?

4. What cities are especially famous for conflict during the civil rights movement? Is Chicago among them?

5. *A Raisin in the Sun* emphasizes that the Youngers' apartment is in Chicago's south side. What can you learn about that section of the city?

6. How can the play itself be seen as part of the civil rights movement?

7. Do you think the events in the play could happen today? Why or why not?

Lesson 8
Act 3

Objectives

- To analyze the play's resolution

- To apply the terms *static, dynamic, round,* and *flat* to the characters

Notes to the Teacher

The final act brings *A Raisin in the Sun* to a quick close. Asagai arrives to visit Beneatha and hears about the dramatic turn of events. Beneatha has become disillusioned about becoming a doctor, and she is furious at Walter. Her idealism seems to have collapsed, and she predicts that Asagai's dreams for Nigeria will also fail. He remains idealistic and goes on to propose marriage, but Beneatha is not ready to answer.

Meanwhile, Walter has decided to accept Mr. Lindner's offer to purchase the house with some profit to the Youngers. Mama grieves the loss of her children's dreams. Somehow, by the time Lindner arrives, Walter has changed his mind. At the end, the Youngers, strengthened by their pride and Walter's decision, decide to face the challenges of a new neighborhood as a united group.

In this lesson, students complete an oral reading of the act. They then complete a study guide and vocabulary exercise; finally, they work with character analysis.

Procedure

1. Have students perform an oral reading of act 3. Roles include Asagai, Beneatha, Ruth, Mama, Walter, Travis, and Mr. Lindner.

2. Distribute **Handout 17**, and have small groups complete the study guide.

    Suggested Responses:

    1. *The story about Rufus's awful sledding accident explains Beneatha's decision to become a doctor.*

    2. *She expresses a loss of her earlier idealism and is cynical about everything. She even mocks Asagai's dreams. At this point, Beneatha has no more dreams.*

    3. *Asagai is very hopeful about his country, but he admits the possibilities Beneatha suggests. He seems to feel there is great promise, and the dangers are not enough to deter him.*

    4. *Asagai wants Beneatha to go to Nigeria with him. He proposes marriage, but Beneatha is not ready to think about that at this point.*

    5. *Beneatha is furious at Walter, practically to the point of disowning him as her brother. Her contempt is obvious: "That is nothing but a toothless rat."*

    6. *Mama has decided not to move to the new house. She is ready to unpack everything and to try to find some ways to improve the apartment.*

    7. *Walter refers to Mr. Lindner. Walter plans to get Lindner to give them a substantial amount of money so that they will not move into the white neighborhood.*

    8. *Mama believes in unconditional love. At this point she is deeply concerned about her family; she feels a great gap between the new generation and those that preceded them.*

    9. *Walter abruptly decides that the family will keep the house. Mama sees the decision as an indication that he has finally left boyhood for maturity, "kind of like a rainbow after the rain."*

    10. *Mama reenters to get her plant and then exits to end the play.*

3. Distribute **Handout 18**, and have students complete the vocabulary exercise. Invite volunteers to share their original sentences.

    Suggested Responses:

    1. ominous—*threatening*

    2. entrepreneur—*person who starts a business*

    3. eludes —*evades*

    4. groveling—*putting oneself in an extremely humble position*

5. trek—*long and difficult journey*

6. reverie—*daydream*

7. precariously—*dangerously*

8. stifle—*repress; hold back*

4. Use **Handout 19** to review the terminology often used to discuss characters. Then ask students to complete the chart by checking the appropriate columns for each character. Conduct a discussion based on their responses.

Suggested Responses:

1. Mama is a major and round character, but not particularly dynamic. From beginning to end her main focus is the well-being of the family. She does change in the amount of responsibility she entrusts to her son.

2. Walter is major, dynamic, and round. As Mama says, the actions in the play facilitate his manhood, as he takes responsibility instead of just indulging in self-pity.

3. Beneatha is major, dynamic, and round. Her disillusionment in act 3 is pretty radical. Still, as we see her chatting about Asagai's proposal near the end, we sense that her depression may not have been as deep as it sounded.

4. Ruth has a fair amount of time on stage, but is a less major character. She is not particularly complex, and she does not seem to change much, although she holds on to the desire to move after the others have given up.

5. Travis is a minor, static, flat character who plays a purely supportive role.

6. Asagai is between major and minor—certainly not as important to the action as Walter, but more important than Travis. He is static; an actor portraying the role can make him look either flat or round.

7. Murchison is fairly minor and very static and flat.

8. Johnson is minor, static, and flat—the busybody.

9. Lindner is minor, static, and flat—the white bigot who really does not understand what is going on.

10. Bobo is minor, flat, and static.

5. Point out that all types of characters are essential to a successful play production. Sometimes an actor who plays a minor role can "steal the show" by doing such a good job with lines and gestures.

Name_____

Date_____

Study Guide: Act 3 of *A Raisin in the Sun*

Directions: Use the following questions to clarify your understanding of the final act.

1. Why does Beneatha tell the story about Rufus?

2. How does Beneatha seem to have changed as a result of Walter's loss of the money?

3. Describe Asagai's attitude toward Nigeria.

4. What does Asagai ask Beneatha to do? How does she respond?

5. What words would describe Beneatha's attitude toward Walter?

6. What does Mama seem to have decided to do?

7. What does Walter mean when he refers to "The Man"? What does Walter plan to do?

8. Explain Mama's comments about love and about all of the work she and her husband did.

9. What surprising decision does Walter make? How does Mama interpret it?

10. What is the last action we see on the stage?

Name_____

Date_____

Act 3: Vocabulary Development

Directions: The final act of *A Raisin in the Sun* is very short and introduces only a few additional words for vocabulary study. Use both context and a dictionary to define the following terms. Then create an original sentence using each one.

Word	Definition	Original Sentence
1. ominous		
2. entrepreneur		
3. eludes		
4. groveling		
5. trek		
6. reverie		
7. precariously		
8. stifle		

Name_____

Date_____

A Look at Characterization

Directions: Review the following terms often used to discuss characters. Then use the chart below to analyze each of the characters in *A Raisin in the Sun*.

- A *major character* has a very important role and spends quite a lot of time on stage.
- A *minor character* plays a supportive role. Characters can be more or less major or minor.
- A *dynamic character* changes in some significant way; the change can be either positive or negative. A character who matures is dynamic, and so is a character who deteriorates.
- A *static character* remains essentially the same as he or she was at the beginning. Characters can be more or less dynamic or static.
- A *round character* is complex, as real people are.
- A *flat character* is one-dimensional; two or three words are often enough to describe a flat character. Characters can be more or less flat or round.

Character	Major	Minor	Dynamic	Static	Round	Flat
1. Mama						
2. Walter						
3. Beneatha						
4. Ruth						
5. Travis						
6. Asagai						
7. Murchison						
8. Johnson						
9. Lindner						
10. Bobo						

Lesson 9
Themes and Symbols

Objectives
- To identify and explain themes in *A Raisin in the Sun*
- To understand the symbolism of Mama's plant
- To consider additional aspects of the play that have symbolic overtones

Notes to the Teacher

Lorraine Hansberry's relatively simple play conveys numerous themes and reinforces traditional values. Students begin this lesson by brainstorming about themes and then focus on articulating theme statements. One of these, the importance of dreams, has been a focus throughout this unit. Students also consider the play's commentary about subjects such as self-respect, materialism, communication, and the strength of the human spirit.

Students then consider the symbols. Mama's plant is the primary symbol in the play. Feeble and small, it has little opportunity to grow in the dim apartment. Mama tends it carefully, though, and the last action we see in the play is her return to fetch the plant for the move to the new house. Several other items in the play carry symbolic overtones. Examples include the Nigerian attire Asagai gives Beneatha, Beneatha's hair, the raisin in the title, and the insurance money.

Procedure
1. Ask students to define the term *theme*, and help them to differentiate between a theme and a topic. Lead them to see that topics are usually neutral, but themes are statements or implications about life, reality, or human nature.

2. Ask the class to brainstorm a list of topics that are central to *A Raisin in the Sun*. Possibilities abound and are likely to include personal dreams, racial relationships, communication, materialism, and other subjects that the class has discussed while studying the play.

3. Distribute **Handout 20**, and have small groups complete the exercise.

Suggested Responses:

1. *Personal dreams dominate the play. Mama dreams of a happier family in the new house, Walter dreams of success and prestige through the liquor business, Beneatha dreams of becoming a doctor, Ruth dreams of a renewed marriage, and Asagai dreams of being part of a new Nigeria. The play shows dreams as sources of meaning and motivation; it also shows that frustrated dreams can cause anger and depression.*

2. *The human spirit at its best seems to be exemplified by Mama, who shows the capacity to endure and to love no matter what happens.*

3. *Communication problems do occur among the characters, who sometimes seem to struggle to make themselves understood. Walter shows that selfishness and self-pity interfere with communication.*

4. *Mama's comments in act 3, after Beneatha says "there is nothing left to love" in Walter, summarize the theme. Love is unconditional; we sometimes need love the most when we least deserve it.*

5. *Racial prejudice is evident in Mr. Lindner's efforts to dissuade the Younger family from moving into Clybourne Park. The play clearly sees bigotry as evil.*

6. *Materialism is exemplified by George Murchison, who is judged a fool by Beneatha. When Asagai calls Beneatha "Alaiyo," he is complimenting her as a person for whom material things are not enough. In the play, what people own is far less important than who they are and the quality of their relationships.*

7. *Frustration leads Walter to anger and self-pity. Near the end, it seems to lead to the collapse of Beneatha's idealism. As disappointed as Mama is, she does not allow frustration to cripple her. Perhaps the play indicates the need for the maturity to cope with frustration.*

8. *Beneatha and Walter are both searching somewhat blindly for self-fulfillment, a trait that Mama seems to have found by not focusing mainly on herself. The play suggests that people find fulfillment by looking beyond their own needs and desires.*

9. *The insurance check is the cause of all of the action in the play. The play seems to indicate that money provides opportunities but promises no success.*

10. *In the play Asagai's idealism is far more attractive than George Murchison's pragmatic approach. Beneatha is more appealing as an idealist than as the disillusioned girl we see early in act 3. Mama is more realist than idealist, but she is certainly not pragmatic. The play suggests the need for idealism to be shored up with a realistic spirit.*

4. If you have been using a plant as a prop in your classroom, invite the class to look at it. Ask them if they think Mama's plant is similar. Point out that the plant is not just an image in the play; it is a symbol. Clarify by pointing out examples. For example, the American flag is not just a piece of cloth with stars and stripes; it symbolizes patriotism and loyalty.

5. Distribute **Handout 21**, and have small groups complete part A.

Suggested Responses:

1. *In act 1, scene 1, when Mama first enters, we see the plant is not at all hardy, but Hansberry uses the phrase "growing doggedly." Despite its environment, the plant does not shrivel up and die.*

2. *At the end of act 1, scene 1, we find that Mama loves the frail little plant, which in a way stands in for the garden that Mama never had.*

3. *When Beneatha implies that Mama should leave "that raggedy-looking old thing" behind, Mama asserts, "It expresses ME!" Like the plant, Mama has gone doggedly on with her life despite disappointments.*

4. *At the end Mama comes back onto the stage for the plant, which has nearly been left behind. The plant is a rich symbol with various interpretations. It represents the capacity to endure, the past that we always take with us into the future, and dreams that never entirely fade away.*

6. Use part B of the handout as the basis of large or small group discussion.

Suggested Responses:

1. *the struggle between assimilationism and ethnic pride*

2. *the desire and effort to smooth things out, to avoid conflict*

3. *opportunity, probably a once-in-a-lifetime chance*

4. *pride in African cultural background*

5. *a dream that withers away*

6. *a false ideal or goal*

7. *opportunity, but also challenges and possible danger*

8. *everything trapped in the city*

9. *search for freedom and meaning*

10. *For example, students may mention characters' names and the music alluded to in the play.*

48

Name_____

Date_____

A Look at Themes

Directions: Each of the topics listed below is important in *A Raisin in the Sun*. Consider each item carefully, and compose a statement that expresses Lorraine Hansberry's theme about that subject. Then list textual evidence that supports your idea.

Topic	Theme	Textual Evidence
1. Personal dreams		
2. The human spirit		
3. Communication		
4. Love		
5. Racial prejudice		

Topic	Theme	Textual Evidence
6. Materialism		
7. Frustration		
8. Self-fulfillment		
9. Money		
10. Idealism		

Mama's Plant and Other Symbols

Part A.

Directions: Mama's plant is an important symbol in *A Raisin in the Sun.* Look again at various times when it is mentioned, and record your observations in the chart below.

Reference	What Happens?	What Does It Mean?
1. Act 1, scene 1, when Mama first enters		
2. The end of act 1, scene 1		
3. Act 2, scene 3, when Mama prepares the plant for the move		
4. The end of act 3		

Part B.

Directions: Comment on the symbolic aspects of each of the following; then identify and explain one other thing you see as symbolic.

1. Beneatha's hair

2. Ruth's ironing

3. The insurance check

4. The Nigerian gown and headpiece

5. A raisin in the sun

6. The liquor store

7. Clybourne Park

8. The rat in act 1, scene 2

9. The trips Walter describes in act 2, scene 2

10. Other: _____

Lesson 10
Structure and Staging

Objectives

- To analyze the play's plot structure
- To focus on the play as a staged event

Notes to the Teacher

Traditionally we see plot structure in segments. First comes the exposition, essentially an introduction to the setting, characters, and basic situation. Rising action follows as a conflict or multiple conflicts develop. Sometimes there is a crisis, or serious turning point. The climax is the highest point of action. The conclusion is variously referred to as resolution, falling action, or denouement. In this lesson, students use these terms to analyze *A Raisin in the Sun*.

They then return to a topic touched on in Lessons 2 and 3, staging. Playwrights seldom see their work solely or even primarily as literature. Lorraine Hansberry's play is meant to be performed. Students address multiple aspects of stage performances and share their work in class presentations.

For procedure 11, you will need art paper or newsprint and markers.

Procedure

1. Ask students, working individually, to list in order the main events in *A Raisin in the Sun*. Clarify by explaining that you want main events only—occurrences that are vital to the play as a whole. After about five minutes, have students meet in small groups to compare and contrast lists.

2. Through whole class discussion, create a list of these major events.

   Suggested Responses:

   - *The insurance check arrives.*
   - *Mama puts a down payment on a house.*
   - *Walter accuses Mama of butchering his dreams.*
   - *Mama entrusts $6,500 to Walter.*
   - *Mr. Lindner tries to talk the Youngers out of moving to Clybourne Park.*
   - *Bobo brings the news that Willy has run off with the money.*

   - *Walter decides that the family will pull together and move to Clybourne Park after all.*

3. Distribute **Handout 22**, and review the diagram with students. Then ask them to fill in items that are part of the play's exposition. (*Five people representing three generations in an African-American family live in a cramped apartment in the south side of Chicago. The time is post–World War II. The furnishings are faded and worn.*)

4. Ask students to identify the central source of conflict in the play as a whole (*the $10,000 life insurance check*).

5. Ask students to identify the first major steps in the rising action. (*Walter walks out at the end of act 1 instead of communicating with his wife and his mother; Mama puts a down payment on the house.*)

6. Tell students that a crisis does occur in this play, one that changes Mama's way of thinking. Ask students to identify it on the diagram. (*Walter accuses Mama of butchering his dreams.*)

7. Ask students to fill in the rest of the rising action and the climax. (*Mama entrusts $6,500 to Walter, who gives it to Willy as an investment in the liquor store. Mr. Lindner tries to talk the family out of the move. The climax occurs when Bobo brings the news that Willy has run off with the money.*)

8. Ask students to use the diagram to summarize the play's resolution. (*Mama resigns herself to having to stay in the apartment; Walter decides that the family will move to Clybourne Park after all. The Youngers leave the apartment, and Mama takes the plant with her.*)

9. Remind students that, at the very beginning of their study of the play, they looked at set design and costuming. Point out that most people who write plays do not think of them as books to be read. Instead, they visualize stage or film productions. On the page, plays can seem a little flat and dull. It takes people, both on stage and in the background, to bring plays to life.

10. Distribute **Handout 23**, and review the information with students. Then use the four questions to prompt students to think about theatrical choices.

   Suggested Responses:

   1. *The director might place a high priority on eliciting audience empathy with the characters.*

   2. *The shabby apartment is not an enthralling sight!*

   3. *This is an apartment, so there might be sounds from other apartments—doors slamming, raised voices, etc. We might hear car horns or train whistles from outside. Dance music is needed for act 2, scene 3.*

   4. *When Walter walks out, should the stage go into complete darkness? Should a shaft of light illuminate Mama's face at the very end?*

11. Divide the class into six groups, and assign each group one of the roles listed on **Handout 23**. Give each group a large sheet of newsprint or art paper, and provide markers or colored pencils. Direct the groups to divide the paper into six sections, one for each scene in the play, and to record the decisions they would make for their area of responsibility for each scene. Encourage students to be creative as they think of ways that the stage can enhance appreciation of the play. When groups have finished their work, have them share ideas with the class as a whole.

Name_____

Date_____

Plot Analysis

Part A.

Directions: Read the following information.

To analyze the plot of any story, we look for several elements.

- The *exposition*, like an introduction, simply presents the basic situation and characters.
- The *rising action* consists of the development and escalation of a conflict or multiple conflicts.
- Sometimes there is a *crisis*, when something happens that shifts the entire direction of events.
- The *climax* is the highest point of action.
- Everything after the climax is *resolution* or *denouement*, as the story comes to a close.

Part B.

Directions: The following diagram shows one way to represent a plot analysis. Fill it in with information about *A Raisin in the Sun*.

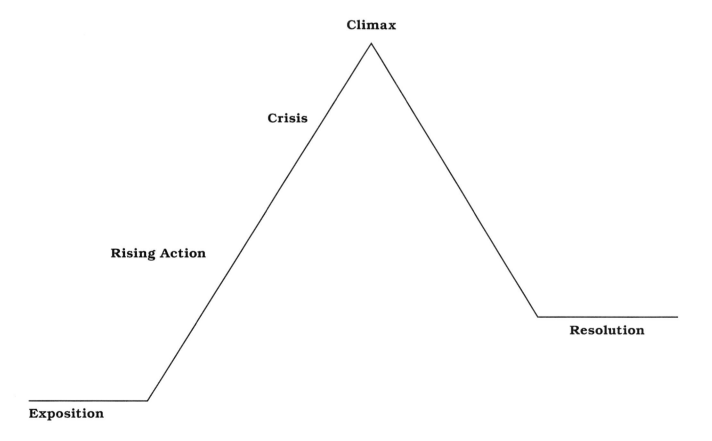

Name_____

Date_____

Staging a Play

Directions: Read the following descriptions of responsibilities involved in staging a play, and answer the questions that follow.

Director—The director is the boss of the show, the main decision-maker. The director chooses the actors and delegates responsibilities to other people. In effect, the director is like an orchestra conductor, responsible for making sure that a lot of other people do their jobs well. The director has a central vision of the show that governs all of his or her choices.

Actors—These are the men and women—and sometimes animals—who perform roles on stage. Actors have to identify with the roles they play and make the characters believable to the audience.

Set designer—This person or team is responsible for what the audience members see on stage throughout the play. The set designer may need people to move items between scenes and may need a prop crew to make sure all of the actors have what they need to make the play a success.

Sound crew—Usually an audience hears more than just actors' voices. There might be music, or sounds might come from the world outside of the stage set. The sound crew is responsible for that.

Costume designers—These people design all of the apparel the actors wear during the performance. They also make sure the clothes fit and stay in good repair.

Light crew—These people are responsible for the amount and quality of light on the stage and around the theater.

1. What might be a director's main desire in staging *A Raisin in the Sun*?

2. What challenges would a set designer face?

3. What sounds might be in the background of the production?

4. Are there any points in the play at which unusual dark or light would be effective?

Lesson 11
"I Have a Dream": Connections

Objectives

- To read, respond to, and analyze Dr. Martin Luther King Jr.'s famous speech

- To connect his themes with themes in *A Raisin in the Sun*

- To read and appreciate other works by African-American writers

Notes to the Teacher

Few other speeches in American history have had the impact of Dr. King's speech during the 1963 March on Washington. His stirring rhetoric and powerful voice proclaimed the mission to make equal civil rights a reality. In this lesson, students read and analyze all or part of the speech, which is readily available online. The speech also appears in *I Have a Dream: Writings and Speeches That Changed the World*, a collection of King's work edited by James Melvin Washington (HarperCollins, 1992). Students then relate the "I Have a Dream" speech to Lorraine Hansberry's play.

The days when literature courses consisted almost solely of pieces from a canon of "dead white men" are over, but, depending on their backgrounds, students may be unaware of the many hugely talented African-American writers who are part of the American literary tradition. The lesson concludes by directing students to research and writing.

Procedure

1. Write the phrase, "I Have a Dream," on the board, and ask students if they recognize it. If necessary, provide information about Dr. Martin Luther King Jr., and explain why we celebrate a January school holiday in his honor.

2. Distribute **Handout 24**, and ask students to read the information about King.

3. Provide copies of the "I Have a Dream" speech, or have students look it up on the Internet. Distribute **Handout 25**, and ask students to read the speech and answer the questions.

   ### Suggested Responses:

   1. *He repeats the phrases "I have a dream" and "Let freedom ring."*

   2. *Children of former slave-owners and slaves will be like brothers and sisters. People will be judged by character, not color. Even states like Mississippi and Alabama will provide equal rights.*

   3. *He refers to many different parts of the country, probably to invite everyone to be part of his movement for equality.*

   4. *He mentions the basic rights guaranteed by the Constitution.*

   5. *He himself calls it a dream, so it is idealistic, but King took realistic steps to bring the dream closer to a reality.*

   6. *Joseph Asagai voices the same energetic idealism.*

   7. *They would recognize their action in buying the house as part of the same dream that Dr. King articulates. Walter and Beneatha would probably be very stirred by the speech; perhaps Travis, now a young man, would be skeptical about the nonviolent approach; Mama and Ruth would probably recognize and appreciate his sincerity and commitment.*

   8. *They both advocate the ability to pursue a better lifestyle without racial prejudice or bigotry. King goes beyond the play in his plea for actual brotherhood and community.*

4. Tell students that the American literary heritage includes great black writers, and many of them have dealt with themes similar to those in the play and in the speech. Assign students to research the work of another African-American author and to write essays in which they relate his or her work to *A Raisin in the Sun*. You may want to choose from the following list, based on students' ages and ability levels.

   - Maya Angelou
   - James Baldwin
   - Toni Cade Bambara
   - Gwendolyn Brooks
   - Countee Cullen

- Frederick Douglass
- Rita Dove
- Paul Laurence Dunbar
- Mari Evans
- Ralph Ellison
- Ernest Gaines
- Alex Haley
- Robert Hayden
- Langston Hughes
- Zora Neale Hurston
- James McBride
- Claude McKay
- Toni Morrison
- August Wilson
- Alice Walker
- Richard Wright

Name_____

Date_____

Dr. Martin Luther King Jr.

Directions: Read the following information about a man who had a great dream about America.

Dr. Martin Luther King Jr., a hero to blacks and whites throughout the world, personifies a man with a vision. Before becoming a Baptist minister, he studied at Crozier Theological Seminary and received a doctoral degree at Boston University. There he met his future wife, Coretta Scott, a music student at the Boston Conservatory of Music. She had no desire to become the wife of a Southern minister but was won over by the effervescence and charm of Martin.

King became involved early in the fight for civil rights for blacks. His first crusade began in 1955, when he led a bus boycott in Alabama to protest the discrimination against black passengers, who were required to ride in the rear of the buses. Due to King's leadership advocating cooperation and nonviolence, the buses became desegregated little more than a year later.

Dr. King led sit-ins, marches, and demonstrations in all parts of the country. Although he and other leaders faced many injustices—arrests, police brutality, violence—he persevered in his crusade and in his philosophy, which was based on the principles of Christianity, the ideas of Henry David Thoreau, and the philosophy of Mahatma Gandhi.

The greatest success King experienced was the dynamic March on Washington in 1963. More than two hundred thousand people paraded to the Lincoln Memorial, where he delivered his famous "I Have a Dream" speech. The march and speech were instrumental in Congress's passing the Civil Rights Act of 1964 and the Voting Rights Act of 1965. King was also honored with the 1964 Nobel Peace Prize.

King was committed to nonviolence, but he and his family were often targets of abuse. While in Memphis to lead striking sanitation workers in April 1968, he was assassinated as he was speaking to friends on the balcony of his hotel room.

Although he did not live to see all of his dreams fulfilled, Dr. Martin Luther King Jr. left a great legacy of commitment to the dream of not only equality, but also genuine community.

Name_____

Date_____

"I Have a Dream"

Directions: When he led the 1963 March on Washington, Dr. Martin Luther King Jr. delivered a famous speech with the refrain, "I have a dream." Read the speech, and answer the following questions.

1. King uses the rhetorical device of repetition. What phrases does he repeat? Why?

2. What are some concrete visions in his dream?

3. To what parts of America does he refer? Why?

4. What basic rights does he mention?

5. Does his dream seem idealistic or realistic? Explain.

6. What character in *A Raisin in the Sun* would be most likely to give a speech like this one?

7. Imagine that the Younger family were present when Dr. King gave this speech. How do you think each would respond?

8. What themes do the play and the speech have in common?

Lesson 12
Looking Backward and Forward

Objectives
- To conjecture about the characters' pre-play experiences
- To forecast events that might occur after the move to Clybourne Park

Notes to the Teacher
This lesson invites students to think about reasons for the main characters' actions. Walter is a relatively young man, a father and a husband who has a low-level menial job as a chauffeur. He is in effect a servant to a white man, and he lives in his mother's apartment. Why is he in this situation? Ruth seems to be trapped in the same position. Why? Unlike her brother, Beneatha is pursuing higher education; she aspires to be a doctor. What causes her to aim so far beyond what the rest of the family have accomplished in their careers? Mama lives in the same apartment she and her husband took many years ago; she seems content to have her daughter and her son and his family live with her. Why? These situations are far from anomalous, and students are quick to see ways that people they know have had similar experiences.

Students then think about events that could occur in a sequel to *A Raisin in the Sun*. Will Walter go back to his job as a chauffeur? Does he have any other options? What has he learned from his sad experience with Willy? Will Ruth become more and more like Mama as she ages? Will Beneatha continue to pursue her medical studies? Will she begin a whole new life with Asagai in Nigeria? Will Mama continue to encourage Walter to be the family decision-maker? Will she be happy in the new house? Will the family be accepted in their new neighborhood?

Procedure
1. Point out that many experiences and events that have made the characters what they are occurred before the time present of the play. Some of them we know—e.g., the recent death of Walter Sr. Others we can only conjecture. Invite brief discussion on factors that led Walter to his situation. He is about thirty years old; his son is ten or eleven; he has a low-level, dead-end job. How did he end up this way? Indicate that we can ask similar questions about the other characters.

2. Divide the class into small groups, and assign one of the main characters to each group. Distribute **Handout 26**, and review the directions. When groups have finished, have them present results to the class as a whole. Results may vary widely, but are likely to include some of the following ideas:
   - Walter became a father at a very young age; this may have interrupted any plans he had for further education. Through most of the play we see him as self-centered and somewhat irresponsible; perhaps he never was very serious about school.
   - Ruth, too, became a parent at a very young age; what attracted her to Walter? Why didn't she ever seek training for a better job?
   - Beneatha grew up in the same household as Walter, but is ten years younger. How did her birth affect him? What kind of role model was he? Was she a good student?
   - Mama indicates that Walter Sr. was not always an easy man with whom to live. What does she mean? What drew her to him in a relationship that lasted many years? What struggles did she have during Walter's and Beneatha's growing-up years? What experiences made Mama into the strong and loving woman she is?

3. Point out that even though *A Raisin in the Sun* was written half a century ago in a very different interracial climate than ours today, much about the characters' situations is timeless. Some children continue to live in their parents' homes long after they should have gone off to become responsible for themselves. Some young people marry and become parents at a very early age, before they have time and opportunity to plan for a successful and fulfilling future.

4. Explain that just as we can inquire into past events before the action in the play, we can also predict about the future. Distribute **Handout 27**, and review the directions. Have students complete the writing assignment either individually or with partners. When they have finished, have them share results in small groups or with the whole class.

Planning an Interview

Part A.

Directions: Conduct a thorough investigation of the pre-play experiences of the character assigned to you. First record the facts. What does Lorraine Hansberry reveal directly? Then conjecture about other events the character is likely to have experienced.

The Facts	Conjectures

Part B.

Directions: Assign one person in the group to play the role of the character. The other students will be interviewers. Create both the questions and the answers. Include topics such as family life, friendships, special interests, educational background, and personal philosophy of life. Then prepare to role-play the interview for the rest of the class.

Name_____

Date_____

A Peek into the Future

Directions: What do you think will happen to the Younger family after their move to Clybourne Park? Will they be happy? Will the neighbors reject them? Use one of the following creative writing topics to explore your ideas. Prepare to present the results to the class as a whole.

1. Write a scene showing events immediately after the play, as the Youngers and the moving van arrive at the new house in Clybourne Park. Include both dialogue and stage directions.

2. Write a scene that shows Mama working in her new garden and chatting with people who pass by, perhaps family members, perhaps neighbors. Include both dialogue and stage directions.

3. Write a scene in which Ruth returns home with the new baby. Include the whole family. Include both dialogue and stage directions.

4. Write a dialogue between Walter and Ruth as they sit on the porch of the new house on a warm summer evening about a year after the move.

5. Imagine that you are a reporter for a Chicago newspaper, and you hear that the Younger family has made the rather unusual decision to move into an all-white neighborhood. Research the facts, and write a human-interest story for your paper.

6. Where will Travis be and what will he be doing ten years later, when he is twenty or twenty-one? Write a story about him.

7. Imagine that you are Beneatha ten years later, when she is about thirty years old. Where is she, and what is she doing? Write a letter home to Mama describing your daily life.

8. Write a scene in which Mrs. Johnson comes to visit Mama in the new house at the same time that Mr. Lindner also stops by. Include both dialogue and stage directions.

Name_____

Date_____

Unit Test

Part A.

Directions: Choose the best response for each of the following items.

_____ 1. *A Raisin in the Sun* is set in
    a. Boston.
    b. New York City.
    c. Chicago.
    d. Detroit.

_____ 2. Mama's first name is
    a. Lena.
    b. Helen.
    c. Melinda.
    d. Karen.

_____ 3. Walter works as a
    a. mechanic.
    b. chauffeur.
    c. chef.
    d. teacher.

_____ 4. Beneatha aspires to be a
    a. nurse.
    b. social worker.
    c. civil engineer.
    d. doctor.

_____ 5. Joseph Asagai is a student from
    a. South Africa.
    b. Nigeria.
    c. Indonesia.
    d. Canada.

_____ 6. Walter would like to open a
    a. pet shop.
    b. gas station.
    c. fast-food restaurant.
    d. liquor store.

_____ 7. Ruth struggles with an inner conflict about
    a. her faith in God.
    b. her hatred for her job.
    c. her pregnancy.
    d. her low self-esteem.

_____ 8. Travis is about
    a. five years old.
    b. eleven years old.
    c. sixteen years old.
    d. twenty years old.

_____ 9. Beneatha finds George Murchison to be
  a. hateful.
  b. lovable.
  c. a racist.
  d. superficial.

_____ 10. Joseph Asagai gives Beneatha
  a. an engagement ring.
  b. clothing.
  c. a job recommendation.
  d. flowers and candy.

_____ 11. Joseph Asagai criticizes Beneatha's
  a. interest in the theater.
  b. study habits.
  c. hair style.
  d. relationship with George Murchison.

_____ 12. Travis gives Mama
  a. a gardening hat.
  b. garden gloves.
  c. a new plant.
  d. a Mother's Day card.

_____ 13. Mama buys a house in
  a. Whitestone Village.
  b. Manor Estates.
  c. Clybourne Park.
  d. Valley Springs.

_____ 14. Who tries to convince the family not to move?
  a. Asagai
  b. the mayor
  c. Mr. Lindner
  d. no one

_____ 15. Who tells Walter that the money has all been stolen?
  a. Bobo
  b. Willy
  c. Randy
  d. Mr. Lindner

_____ 16. The rising action of the play is based on
  a. an inheritance.
  b. lottery winnings.
  c. money that Mama has earned.
  d. a life insurance policy.

_____ 17. The most dynamic character in the play is
  a. Mama.
  b. Ruth.
  c. Beneatha.
  d. Walter.

Name_____

Date_____

_____ 18. A central symbol is
    a. Mama's wedding ring.
    b. a houseplant.
    c. an old clock.
    d. a picture of a river.

_____ 19. The title of the play emphasizes the importance of
    a. personal dreams.
    b. faith in God.
    c. ethnic heritage.
    d. an optimistic spirit.

_____ 20. At the end of the play, the family has decided to
    a. stay in the apartment.
    b. move to the house Mama bought.
    c. move to Africa.
    d. buy a less expensive house.

Part B.

Directions: Choose the best response for each of the following statements.

_____ 1. A person who is overly proud and self-satisfied can be described as
    a. exuberant.
    b. ludicrous.
    c. arrogant.
    d. quizzical.

_____ 2. A person who seems threatening and dangerous is
    a. forlorn.
    b. furtive.
    c. coquettish.
    d. menacing.

_____ 3. A disaster is
    a. a cliché.
    b. an incredulity.
    c. a catastrophe.
    d. an indictment.

_____ 4. A reverie is a
    a. photograph album.
    b. nostalgic song.
    c. prayer book.
    d. daydream.

_____ 5. The sound of an ambulance siren is
    a. strident.
    b. plaintive.
    c. amiable.
    d. tentative.

_____ 6. Someone who is very weak is
   a. raucous.
   b. feeble.
   c. futile.
   d. forlorn.

_____ 7. Someone who experiences anguish is
   a. in great pain.
   b. in love for the first time.
   c. quarrelsome.
   d. exuberant.

_____ 8. An entrepreneur is a
   a. medical student.
   b. businessman.
   c. social failure.
   d. thief.

_____ 9. A trek is
   a. a motor vehicle.
   b. an old joke.
   c. a type of houseplant.
   d. a long journey.

_____ 10. Someone who is exasperated is
   a. peaceful.
   b. frustrated.
   c. depressed.
   d. cheerful.

Part C.

Directions: Write one or two well-developed paragraphs in response to each of the following prompts.

1. During the course of the play, how and why does Mama's attitude toward her children change?

2. Compare and contrast Joseph Asagai and George Murchison.

3. Identify the dreams of the play's main characters.

4. Explain the significance of the title.

Answer Key

Part A.

1.	c	11.	c
2.	a	12.	a
3.	b	13.	c
4.	d	14.	c
5.	b	15.	a
6.	d	16.	d
7.	c	17.	d
8.	b	18.	b
9.	d	19.	a
10.	b	20.	b

Part B.

1.	c	6.	b
2.	d	7.	a
3.	c	8.	b
4.	d	9.	d
5.	a	10.	b

Part C.

1. Mama realizes that both Beneatha and Walter have had their dreams frustrated, and this grieves her. She relinquishes some of her control in the family to them, especially to Walter, whom she allows to make the final decision about whether or not to move. Throughout the play, Mama's top priority is the well-being of the family as a whole, and she seems to realize the need to empower the younger people to grow into responsible adulthood.

2. Asagai and Murchison are about the same age, and they share a romantic interest in Beneatha. Asagai, however, exudes racial pride and determination to return to Nigeria and be a part of creating a proud new country. He is an intellectual and an idealist. Murchison is an assimilationist, desiring to fit into American culture. He is also pragmatic and materialistic.

3. Mama dreams of a better life for the family, and she focuses this dream on the new house. Walter dreams of escaping his job as a chauffeur, and he focuses on the desire for co-ownership of a liquor store. Beneatha dreams of becoming a doctor as a way to help people. Ruth seems to dream of a renewed marriage with Walter and of a better life out of the crowded apartment.

4. The title alludes to a poem by Langston Hughes. In it, unachieved dreams are compared to things like raisins drying up in the sun and spoiled meat. At the end, the poem suggests that frustrated dreams can lead to violence. Like the poem, the play also focuses on dreams, but Lorraine Hansberry's conclusion indicates that, with determination and love, people can turn dreams into reality.

The Publisher

All instructional materials identified by the TAP® (Teachers/ Authors/Publishers) trademark are developed by a national network of teachers whose collective educational experience distinguishes the publishing objective of The Center for Learning, a nonprofit educational corporation founded in 1970.

Concentrating on values-related disciplines, the Center publishes humanities and religion curriculum units for use in public and private schools and other educational settings. Approximately 500 language arts, social studies, novel/drama, life issues, and faith publications are available.

While acutely aware of the challenges and uncertain solutions to growing educational problems, the Center is committed to quality curriculum development and to the expansion of learning opportunities for all students. Publications are regularly evaluated and updated to meet the changing and diverse needs of teachers and students. Teachers may offer suggestions for development of new publications or revisions of existing titles by contacting

The Center for Learning
10200 Jefferson Blvd.
P.O. Box 802
Culver City, CA 90232-0802
(800) 421-4246 • Fax (800) 944-5432
E-mail: access@centerforlearning.org
Web: www.centerforlearning.org